My Name Is Not Slow
Kids with Intellectual Disabilities

Kids with Special Needs

My Name Is Not Slow
Kids with Intellectual Disabilities

by Sheila Stewart and Camden Flath

MASON CREST PUBLISHERS INC.
370 Reed Road
Broomall, Pennsylvania 19008
(866)MCP-BOOK (toll free)
www.masoncrest.com

First Printing
9 8 7 6 5 4 3 2 1

ISBN (set) 978-1-4222-1727-6   ISBN (pbk set) 978-1-4222-1918-8

Library of Congress Cataloging-in-Publication Data

Stewart, Sheila, 1975–
  My name is not slow : kids with intellectual disabilities / by Sheila Stewart and Camden Flath.
      p. cm.
  Includes bibliographical references and index.
  ISBN 978-1-4222-1718-4   ISBN (pbk) 978-1-4222-1921-8
  1. Children with mental disabilities—Juvenile literature. I. Flath, Camden, 1987– II. Title.

  HQ773.7.S69 2010
  305.23087—dc22
                        2010007063

Produced by Harding House Publishing Service, Inc.
www.hardinghousepages.com
Design by MK Bassett-Harvey.
Cover design by Torque Advertising Design.
Printed in the USA by Bang Printing.

Photo Credits
Creative Commons Attribution 2.0 Generic: jemsweb: pg. 38; National Library of Medicine: pg. 34; San Luis Obispo County, California: pg. 40; United States Army: pg. 29, 43.

The creators of this book have made every effort to provide accurate information, but it should not be used as a substitute for the help and services of trained professionals.

Introduction

To the Teacher

Kids with Special Needs provides a unique forum for demystifying a wide variety of childhood medical and developmental disabilities. Written to captivate an elementary-level audience, the books bring to life the challenges and triumphs experienced by children with common chronic conditions such as hearing loss, intellectual disability, physical differences, and speech difficulties. The topics are addressed frankly through a blend of fiction and fact.

This series is particularly important today as the number of children with special needs is on the rise. Over the last two decades, advances in pediatric medical techniques have allowed children who have chronic illnesses and disabilities to live longer, more functional lives. At the same time, IDEA, a federal law, guarantees their rights to equal educational opportunities. As a result, these children represent an increasingly visible part of North American population in all aspects of daily life. Students are exposed to peers with special needs in their classrooms, through extracurricular activities, and in the community. Often, young people have misperceptions and unanswered questions about a child's disabilities—and more important, his or her abilities. Many times, there is no vehicle for talking about these complex issues in a comfortable manner.

This series will encourage further conversation about these issues. Most important, the series promotes a greater comfort for its readers as they live, play, and study side by side with these children who have medical and developmental differences—kids with special needs.

—*Dr. Carolyn Bridgemohan*
Boston Pediatric Hospital/Harvard Medical School

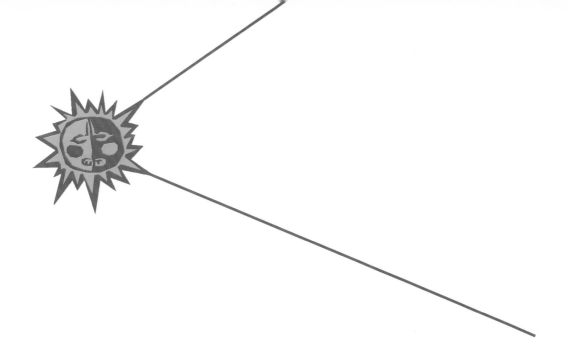

Just as I walk past his seat on the bus, Nick Howard sticks out his foot. I trip and have to grab another seat to keep from falling down.

"Watch where you're walking, Slow!" Nick Howard yells. I do not say anything and I do not look at him as I keep walking and sit down. That's what Mom told me to do.

For as long as I can remember, Nick Howard has been my enemy. He calls me stupid, idiot, dummy, moron, and a lot of other things, but I've never heard him call me "Slow" before. Maybe all those words are true if you look at me a certain way—I know I think and learn more slowly than other kids—but they're *mean*. I don't know why he hates me. I've never done anything to him.

"Ignore him, Trinity," Emma O'Connor says to me when I sit down. Emma is my friend. I sit with her every day on the bus and she is never mean to me.

"That's what I was doing," I say to Emma, and then, I can't help but whisper, "But my name is NOT Slow!"

Emma giggles, which helps me feel better. I don't want to think about Nick Howard anymore, so I tell her about the show I watched on TV last night. The show was about a family of bears living in the woods. Real bears, not cartoon ones.

"I wish I could paint them," I say to Emma, "but I'm too stupid."

"Don't be an idiot," Emma says. "You're not stupid." And then we laugh and laugh.

Emma can make a joke like that because she is my friend and I know that she loves me. Nobody else is allowed to say something like that, though. I like it that Emma treats me like everyone else. Like I'm normal.

The bus stops in front of the school and we get off. Emma is in my class, which is good. Nick Howard is not in my class this year, which is also good.

We go into class and sit down at our desks. Emma sits in front of me, but Mrs. Lewis says that if we talk during class time she will have to separate us. I don't want that to happen. Emma has other friends, like Jessie and Rose, but I mostly just have Emma.

All the other kids are coming in and sitting down, too. I look at them because I like to look at people. People are interesting, even though they don't always make sense. Some of the kids are nice to me and some are mean to me sometimes, but most people just ignore me. Ignoring is better than mean, but sometimes it's still bad.

I see Becky when she walks into the classroom, and I smile and wave at her. Becky is my aide. That means she helps me with my work in class when I need her. She's nice and she's good at explaining stuff so I can understand. Mrs. Lewis is pretty nice, too, but a lot of times I don't understand what she means, even though everyone else seems to understand.

"Good morning, Trinity!" Becky says. "How are you this morning?"

"I'm good," I say. "How is Blinky?" Blinky is Becky's cat.

"Cute as ever," says Becky.

Class is going to start, so Becky goes and sits at her own desk at the back of the room. She usually lets me work by myself unless I'm having trouble. Someday, I will live on my own, and I need to be able to survive without Becky. That's what Dad says. I don't know about living on my own, because I'm only ten. I like living at home with Mom and Dad and Ryan and Sophia. Dad

says that what he means is that something bad happened to me while I was being born so I have to work harder than most people to understand things—and he wants me to be able to manage without the family when I grow up, just like other people do when they're adults.

But I am not a stupid moron, no matter what Nick Howard says.

My favorite class is art. When I was little, Mom and Dad took us to the art museum a lot—that was before Sophia was born. I loved looking at all the pictures and the colors made me happy. Sometimes we still go to the museum, but everybody is busy a lot now.

In art class today Ms. Weber starts to talk about an artist named Picasso. I'm not sure I like Picasso's paintings at first, but then I think it's interesting how he looked at things a little piece at a time. Ms. Weber tells us all to make our own Picasso painting.

I decide that I'm going to paint Emma. I start with her ear, because she's wearing a nice earring with a smiley face. I do her nose and her eye and then her other eye. The best thing about painting like Picasso is that things don't have to line up just right, you can just connect them and say you wanted it to be that way.

I think when I grow up I will be an artist, but first I will have to learn to paint things that line up. You can't paint like Picasso all the time—unless you are Picasso. I will paint like Trinity, because that's me.

After art, we have lunch and then we have science class. In science, we are learning about cells, which are little things that make up your body. Different cells do different things. I understand that, but I don't always remember what the different kinds of cells are or what the things inside the cells are.

Sometimes I think my brain fills up with all the stuff they try to teach me and there isn't enough room for it all. I remember what's important—like stuff about my family and my friends—but cells don't seem very important. So they just slip out of my brain, and then they're gone, and I can't find them again.

Becky says I should think of cells like people, because they're different and have different jobs. I try to do that, but it's still confusing.

It's almost the end of class when Mrs. Lewis says, "Don't forget you're being tested on this on Thursday."

But I *had* forgotten. Today is Tuesday, so that means that Thursday is only two days away. I don't like tests; they're scary and they make me feel stupid.

I start breathing fast because I'm thinking about the test. I turn around and look at Becky. She waves her hands at me like she's saying, *Calm down, Trinity.*

I want to calm down and I don't want to think about tests, so I poke Emma in the back and whisper, "Do you want to sleep over on Friday?" Mrs. Lewis doesn't notice that I'm talking to Emma, which is good.

When I get home from school, Mom looks through my backpack. She looks at the work I did in school today and finds the notebook that Becky and Mrs. Lewis write notes in.

"You have a science test in a couple of days," Mom says, and I frown.

"Oh, yeah," I say. "Can Emma come over on Friday night for a sleepover?"

"No changing the subject," Mom says. "We'll go over the other work you did today, and after supper you can start studying for the science test."

"I don't want to," I say. "I don't care about cells."

But Mom says I have to care about cells, for a while anyway.

After we read over the things I learned in school today, I set the table while Mom makes spaghetti. I put out five plates and put a fork and a knife and a spoon beside every plate. I get out five glasses, and I make sure the princess glass is at Sophia's place and the race-car glass is at Ryan's place. I give the glass with the rabbits to me, and I give Mom and Dad plain red glasses. Ryan tells me he's too old for the racecar glass, but I think he still likes it so I give it to him anyway. He's twelve, and that's only two years older than me.

When supper is over, Mom asks Sophia to help me study for the science test. Sophia is supposed to ask me questions from the study sheet Mrs. Lewis sent. Sophia can't read all the words, though, because she's only six, so Dad helps instead.

"What is the nucleus of a cell?" Dad asks.

I don't know what a nucleus is. I stare at Dad and I'm afraid I will cry.

"Take it easy," he says. "It'll be okay."

"Isn't the nucleus the middle part?" asks Sophia.

I start feeling worse because I don't like being stupid and everybody else is smarter than me. Even my little sister.

Dad sends Sophia to do her own homework, and then he talks to me about cells and explains them and

draws pictures. I start understanding a little bit, but I I'm not sure I'll remember what he's saying by the time I take the test.

Then Dad looks at me and tells me I need a break. "We'll study again tomorrow night," he says. "You can go watch something on TV if you like."

That sounds good to me, so I go and watch a show about a cat who lives in a nursing home and cuddles with people. Maybe, I think, if I'm not an artist, I could look after animals. Or maybe I could do both.

On Thursday, right before Mrs. Lewis starts handing out the test, Becky kneels down beside my desk and makes me look at her eyes.

"Breathe, Trinity," she says. "Take deep breaths. If you start getting worried, close your eyes for a second and take deep breaths. Just do your best and don't worry right now if you get some of the answers wrong."

I try to take deep breaths. I hold my pencil so tight it breaks. Becky takes the pieces of pencil out of my hand and gives me a new one.

"It will be okay," she says. Then she and I go out in the hall. We sit at the desk and Becky reads the questions to me.

I close my eyes and try to breath. Then I open my eyes and look at the test, while Becky reads the first question. "Label the parts of the cell," she says, and there is a drawing of a cell with little lines coming out from it. For a minute the drawing looks like squiggles and blobs, but I make myself breathe and think. I remember Sophia saying what the middle is called. I try hard to hear her voice in my head, so that I can remember the word she said, and after what seems like a long time, it comes to me: "Nucleus!" Becky writes down the word for me on the test paper, because writing and spelling are two of the things that are hard for me.

I shut my eyes again and try to think. I remember Dad drawing other parts of the cell, and I tell Becky the ones I can remember. I can't remember all of them, though.

Becky reads the rest of the questions, one at a time. I try to breathe and listen and think, all at the same time. The other kids come out the door and go to recess, so Becky and I go back into the classroom while I finish the test.

And then, finally, I'm all done, and that's a good thing.

Now that the science test is over, I feel happy. I don't have to think about it anymore. After school, I go over my homework with Mom, but I'm not paying attention to what she says. My brain feels too tired.

When she says we're finished, I go to my room and get out my paints. I paint a picture of me taking the test, with a big squiggly blue cell on the paper in front of me. I get happy like this whenever I take a test and it's done.

The next day, Mrs. Lewis gives back the science tests and all my happy goes away because I'm afraid to look at it. I fold it up without looking and put it in my folder.

If I have a very bad grade, I will be sad, and Mom and Dad will be sad. Once, after I got 17 on a geography test (that's a really, really bad F), I heard Mom crying. She told Dad that she didn't know what to do about me. I felt like my stomach was sick when I heard that. I don't want to make Mom cry.

Becky comes over to my desk. "How did you do on the test, Trinity?" she asks.

"I don't know," I say. "I'm not looking."

"I think you should look."

I look at her eyes. "Okay," I say. I take out the test and unfold it. Then, very slowly, I look down. On the top of the paper, in red pen, it says "75." I take a deep breath.

"75 is good," I say. "It's passing."

"Yes, it is," says Becky. "It's better than passing. I'm proud of you, Trinity."

When I get home, Mom takes the science test and sticks it on the fridge with a magnet shaped like a mouse. She is smiling, and that makes me happy.

"I talked to Emma's mother," Mom says. "She said Emma could sleep over tonight. We'll go and get her after Ryan gets home and we can pick up some pizza and a movie."

That makes me happy, too. I run to my room and clean up so there will be room to put the inflatable bed on the floor. My room can get messy sometimes. By the time I finish clearing off the floor of my room, Ryan is home from middle school.

I get in the van, and Ryan and Sophia get in too. Mom drives to Emma's house, and when we stop in Emma's driveway, she comes running out of her house carrying a purple backpack and a pillow. The pillow has a bright orange pillowcase.

"Hey, Trinity!" she says as she climbs into the van and sits beside me.

I am so happy now that all I can do is smile and smile. My best friend is here and I have no test to worry about for a while. When I am happy like this, I don't care that my brain doesn't work the same as everybody else's. There are some things that are better than being smart, I think.

But then I think about the pictures I make. I think about being Emma's friend and about the way Mom and Dad smile at me. And I think I'm smart, too, it just isn't the same kind of smart as everybody else.

Kids and Intellectual Disabilities

Intellectual disability makes a person's mind work differently from other people's. This disability can make it harder for a child to learn to speak or walk. A child with intellectual disability may have trouble keeping up with kids his own age in school. He may need help learning things that other kids pick up quickly, or he may need help doing things that many kids take for granted. Many children with intellectual disabilities have trouble thinking through problems, making decisions, or understanding *consequences*.

Kids with intellectual disabilities face many *challenges* —but they aren't all that different from other kids. They can be kind people with many skills. They're worth getting to know!

Intellectual has to do with thinking or using your mind.

A *disability* is a problem—either physical or mental— that gets in the way of a person doing what other people can do.

Consequences are things that happen because something else happened first. For example, if you go out in the rain, the consequence will be that you get wet. If you stay up talking all night at a sleepover, the consequence will be that you're sleepy the next day.

Challenges are things that are hard or difficult that must be faced and overcome.

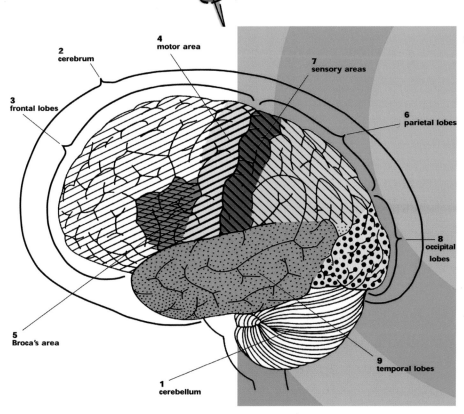

		4 motor area		7 sensory areas	
2 cerebrum					
3 frontal lobes				6 parietal lobes	
				8 occipital lobes	
5 Broca's area				9 temporal lobes	
	1 cerebellum				

Your brain controls the rest of your body. If the brain does not develop properly, it may cause intellectual disability.

Around the world, almost 200 million people have some level of intellectual disability. With so many people with intellectual disabilities, it's important to understand what this disability means.

Develop *means to grow and learn.*

What Is Intellectual Disability?

Intellectual disability causes a person's mind to *develop* more slowly than average. This means that a baby with this disability may not smile until she is nearly a year old, while other babies usually begin to smile when they are only a month or two old. A child may not talk until she is four or five, even though other children usually begin to talk before they are two years old. She may not learn to read until she is ten years old, instead of

six, along with other kids her age. She may never learn to read. The mind of a kid with intellectual disability will never catch up all the way. She will also think and learn more slowly than other people do.

Intellectual disability will make it harder for a kid to take care of himself and *communicate*. He may have trouble speaking correctly, understanding rules, or solving problems. In school, kids with intellectual disabilities may learn new material, but not as quickly as other kids their age. They may have trouble understanding more difficult subjects or ideas. Intellectual disability makes it harder for them to get along with others, walk and run, or think through things the way other kids do.

Intellectual disability was once known as mental retardation. In 2008, the American Association on Intellectual and Developmental Disabilities (AAIDD) recommended that the term be changed from *mental retardation* to intellectual disability. The intellectual disability community decided to use the new term because "mental retardation" was hurtful to many people with this disability. People felt as though the term "mental retardation" carried with it the thought that people with this disability are not worth as much as other people. Today,

> The word **mental** has to do with the mind's abilities.
>
> **Retardation** is a condition where something has been slowed down or kept from going forward.

An intellectual disability can make school difficult for a child. He may not be able to learn as quickly as other students.

the term intellectual disability is widely used in books and by groups working with those who have intellectual disabilities. Many books and laws created before 2008, however, still use the term mental retardation.

What Happens If a Person Has Intellectual Disability?

Each person with intellectual disability is different. Kids with intellectual disabilities will have different abilities in areas of communication, movement, and problem solving. These kids will have to make different changes in their lives to make up for their intellectual disability. Some

An intellectual disability can begin showing up at an early age, when a baby fails to sit up, crawl, or walk at the expected times.

forms of intellectual disability are very serious, which will mean that a person with a serious disability will not be able to do very many things that other people do. Some intellectual disabilities aren't very serious at all, though, and people who have *mild* intellectual disabilities will be able to do most of the things other people do.

Because intellectual disability affects the way a person's mind works and develops, kids with intellectual disabilities may have trouble in many areas of their lives. Kids with intellectual disabilities may:

> *Mild* means not very serious, not very bad.
>
> *Inappropriate* means that something is not the right thing to do at a certain time in a certain place. For example, it would be inappropriate to burp loudly in the middle of class.

- not learn to sit up, crawl, or walk at the same time as other kids their age.
- not learn to talk at the same time as other kids their age. (Kids with intellectual disabilities may also have difficulty speaking once they do learn to speak.)
- have trouble understanding ideas like money or how to pay for things.
- not understand social rules or have difficulty understanding why something they've done is *inappropriate*.

- have difficulty thinking through things. (Kids with intellectual disabilities may have trouble thinking about the consequences of their actions or making decisions based on those consequences.)
- have trouble solving problems.

Not all kids with intellectual disabilities will experience all of these difficulties. Some may only have troubles in a few of these areas.

What Causes Intellectual Disability?

Many different things can cause intellectual disability. A few of the most common causes are:

- *Genetic problems:* Our genes are the maps inside our cells that give the instructions for who we are and who we will become. Genes are passed down to us from our parents. Genes can cause intellectual disability when genes that are damaged or not normal are passed from parents to their kids. Genes from both parents that don't combine correctly can also cause intellectual disability in a child. Conditions like Down syndrome or Fragile X syndrome, two different types of intellectual disabilities, are caused by genetic problems.

- *Problems before birth:* If the baby does not develop correctly before she is born, she may be born with some type of intellectual disability. Certain types of infections a mother gets during pregnancy can cause her baby to be born with intellectual disability. A mother who drinks alcohol or uses drugs while pregnant can also have a baby with intellectual disability.
- *Problems during birth:* Babies who do not get enough oxygen while they are being born can end up with intellectual disabilities.

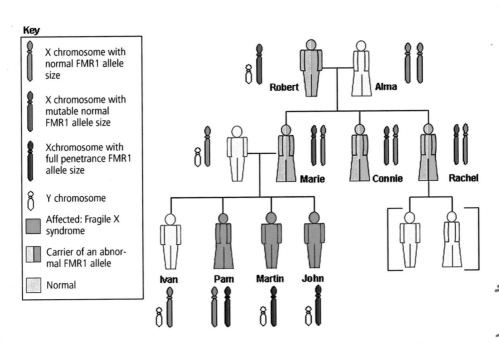

Key

- X chromosome with normal FMR1 allele size
- X chromosome with mutable normal FMR1 allele size
- X chromosome with full penetrance FMR1 allele size
- Y chromosome
- Affected: Fragile X syndrome
- Carrier of an abnormal FMR1 allele
- Normal

Intellectual disability may be caused by genetics. In this example, Robert and Marie carry a genetic problem called Fragile X syndrome, but do not have the disorder. Marie's children, Pam, Martin, and John, all have the syndrome.

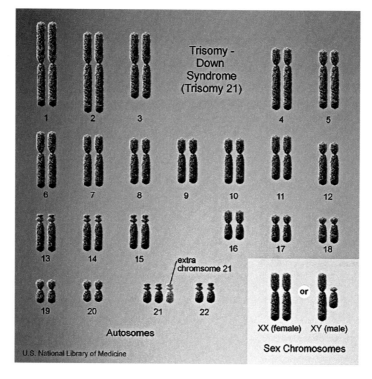

Trisomy - Down Syndrome (Trisomy 21)

1 2 3 4 5
6 7 8 9 10 11 12
13 14 15 16 17 18
19 20 21 22

extra chromsome 21

XX (female) or XY (male)

Autosomes

Sex Chromosomes

U.S. National Library of Medicine

Another intellectual disability caused by genetics is Down syndrome. Also called Trisomy 21, it is caused by an extra chromosome, which is a thread-like structure made up of DNA.

- *Other health problems:* Some diseases can also cause a child to develop an intellectual disability, especially sicknesses that cause very high fevers. If a child is poisoned by being around *lead* or *mercury*, she can also develop intellectual disability.

Diagnosing Intellectual Disabilities

In order to be *diagnosed* as having an intellectual disability, a child must show the three following signs:

1. Intellectual ability far below average.
2. Difficulties with at least two of the following skills:
   - communication
   - social skills
   - self-care
   - home living
   - safety
   - health
   - entertainment or play
   - work
   - learning
   - use of community resources
3. Signs of intellectual disability appear before the age of 18.

Lead is a kind of metal that is found in old paint and water pipes.

Mercury is another kind of metal that because of water pollution can get into fish. Mercury pollution can also get inside other animals and plants. Mercury is also found inside certain kinds of lights, and if they're broken, a person might breathe the mercury.

Diagnosed means that a doctor figured out what was wrong with someone.

If parents think their child might have some level of intellectual disability, a doctor or *psychologist* can do tests. One of these tests is called an IQ test. IQ (which stands for "intelligence quotient") is used as a measurement of how well a child can do in school, solve problems, and make decisions.

We use inches and feet (or meters) to measure length, pounds and ounces (or grams) to measure weight—and IQ is the tool experts use to measure intelligence. But intelligence isn't like length or weight. It can't be measured in the same way. This means that a very low IQ is usually a sign of possible intellectual disability, but IQ tests aren't perfect. It also means that IQ should never be used to measure how much a person is worth! People come in many shapes and sizes. Short people are just as good as tall people, people with brown hair are as nice as people with blonde hair—and people with low IQs are just as interesting and important as people with high IQs.

Since IQ tests aren't always the best way to tell if a person has intellectual disability, doctors and psychologists

A **psychologist** is someone who has studied how the mind and emotions work. She will work with kids and adults in schools and other places to help them understand and handle their feelings and thoughts better.

may also use other tests. They may test a child's **adaptive** behavior, for example. Adaptive behavior is made up of three different types of skills:

- **Conceptual** skills: These cover things like the meaning of words, reading and writing, money, the idea of time, and the meaning of numbers.
- Social skills: These include the way we get along with others, how we feel about ourselves, sharing, and understanding what others are feeling.
- **Practical** skills: Activities like taking care of yourself, understanding safety, being able to use the telephone, and knowing how to stay healthy all fall under the category of practical skills.

> **Adaptive** has to do with our ability to change the way we act and think in order to handle different kinds of things.
>
> **Conceptual** is a word that has to do with ideas.
>
> **Practical** means having to do with everyday things, the ordinary parts of life.

How Is Intellectual Disability Treated?

Intellectual disability is not a disorder or sickness that can be cured. Instead, intellectual disabilities cause long-term and permanent changes in the way a person thinks and how her brain develops. Kids with intellectual disabilities will likely need help in facing these challenges. There are many programs to help children and adults with intellectual disabilities succeed in school, among friends, and at home. Experts who understand the different difficulties caused by intellectual disabilities can help kids and adults learn new skills and improve their abilities in many areas.

A child with intellectual disability may need help learning to dress himself.

The goal of many of the programs for kids with intellectual disabilities is to improve adaptive behavior. This means kids with intellectual disabilities work on language skills, social skills, problem solving, and decision making, as well as many day-to-day skills such as dressing, bathing, and handling money. A kid with intellectual disability might work with a *speech therapist* to help him learn to speak correctly, for example. A lot of this help will be given at a child's school. As kids with intellectual disabilities grow older, they will work on the skills they will need to care for themselves (like going shopping, paying bills, taking a bus, or having a job). Many programs work with people with intellectual disabilities to find jobs, and continue to improve their social skills and day-to-day abilities.

> A *speech therapist* is a person who helps people who have trouble speaking to learn ways to talk more clearly.

Intellectual Disabilities and School

Many kids with intellectual disabilities will be able to succeed in a classroom setting that meets their special needs. Kids with intellectual disability who have trouble speaking, for example, can spend time at school with a speech

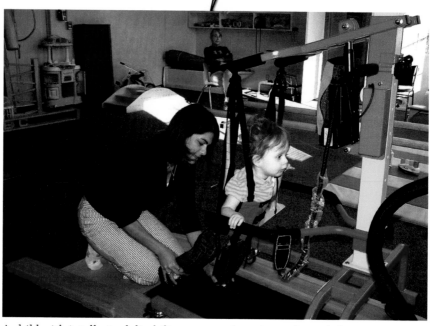

A child with intellectual disability may need to visit a physical therapist to learn how to walk.

therapist. A speech therapist can help a child who has difficulty speaking learn to speak correctly over time. If a child with intellectual disability has a hard time getting along with other kids her age, she can work on her social skills in a special class. Some kids with intellectual disabilities may need help learning to walk; they may need to work on their balance. A physical therapist can help kids with intellectual disabilities learn to walk or stand correctly. An occupational therapist helps children learn small movements, such as hand and finger movements. These experts can help kids with intellectual disabilities get the help that they need in school. For many kids with intellectual disabilities, this kind of *special education* will be the best way to learn important skills and succeed in school.

A law called the Individuals with Disabilities Education Act (IDEA) outlines how schools should decide which kids need special education. In order to *qualify* for special education under IDEA, the child's intellectual disability must get in the way of his learning or taking part in school activities.

The IDEA law lists thirteen different kinds of disabilities that may mean a child will qualify for special education. Mental retardation is one *category* under IDEA. This term has yet to be changed to intellectual disability in the language of the law.

The IDEA law requires that:

> *Special education* teaches kids who have trouble learning because of some disability.
>
> To *qualify* means to fit the definition of something or to meet the requirements.
>
> A *category* is a group or a certain kind of thing.

- the child has problems performing well at school activities.
- the child's parent, teacher, or other school staff person must ask that the child be examined for a disability.

- the child is *evaluated* to decide if she does indeed have a disability and to figure out what kind of special education she needs.
- a group of people, including the kid's parents, teachers, and an expert on intellectual disabilities, meets to decide on a plan for helping him. This plan is called an Individualized Education Program (IEP). The IEP spells out exactly what the child needs in order to succeed at school.

> When something is *evaluated*, it is examined to see in which category it belongs.

Succeeding with Intellectual Disabilities

Parents, brothers, and sisters are also important in the life of a child with intellectual disability. They can help teach the child how to talk and get along with others. Most important, they can help the child feel loved and accepted.

Each person with intellectual disability has a different range of things she can do. But she will not outgrow her disorder. She will have intellectual disability throughout her entire life. But many people with intellectual disabilities can learn to handle the challenges of their disorder. Some may grow up to have jobs that are suited to their

The Special Olympics allows kids with intellectual disability to participate in sports competition.

abilities, and they will be able to live on their own and even raise families. Others will need extra help their whole life. Either way, these people are interesting individuals who are worth getting to know. They know how to love others—and they know and appreciate when they are loved and respected by others.

Kids with intellectual disabilities can do amazing things. They can be great students, athletes, friends, and artists. For example, each year, kids with intellectual disabilities compete in the Special Olympics. Begun in 1968, the Special Olympics is held each year for people with intellectual disabilities to participate in sports competition.

Though kids with intellectual disabilities face many challenges, they can also do great things with the right help and support. You can help build bridges between people you meet who may seem different from yourself by always treating everyone with respect, the way you would want to be treated yourself. Do your part to help those around you succeed and feel like they belong!

Further Reading

Note: Before 2008, the term mental retardation was used for many types of intellectual disabilities. As a result, much of the literature created before 2008 uses the term mental retardation.

Abramovitz, M. *Mental Retardation*. Detroit, Mich.: Lucent Books, 2007.

Bowman-Kruhm, M. *Everything You Need to Know About Down Syndrome*. New York: Rosen Publishing, 2000.

Kennedy, M. *Special Olympics*. Danbury, Conn.: Children's Press, 2002.

Royston, A. *Explaining Down Syndrome*. North Mankato, Minn.: Smart Apple Media, 2009.

Trainer, M. and H. Featherstone. *Differences in Common: Straight Talk on Mental Retardation, Down Syndrome, and Your Life*. Bethesda, Ma.: Woodbine House, 2003.

Zuckoff, M. *Choosing Naia: A Family's Journey*. Boston, Mass.: Beacon Press, 2002.

Find Out More On the Internet

American Association on Intellectual and Developmental Disabilities
www.aaidd.org

The ARC of the United States
www.thearc.org

The Center for an Accessible Society
www.accessiblesociety.org

Inclusion International
www.inclusion-international.org

National Association for Down Syndrome
www.nads.org

National Dissemination Center for Children with Disabilities
www.nichcy.org

National Down Syndrome Society
www.ndss.org

Special Olympics
www.specialolympics.org

Understanding Intellectual Disability & Health
www.intellectualdisability.info

Disclaimer

The websites listed on this page were active at the time of publication. The publisher is not responsible for websites that have changed their address or discontinued operation since the date of publication. The publisher will review and update the websites upon each reprint.

Index

About the Authors

Sheila Stewart has written several dozen books for young people, both fiction and nonfiction, although she especially enjoys writing fiction. She has a master's degree in English and now works as a writer and editor. She lives with her two children in a house overflowing with books, in the Southern Tier of New York State.

Camden Flath is a writer living and working in Binghamton, New York. He has a degree in English and has written several books for young people. He is interested in current political, social, and economic issues and applies those interests to his writing.

About the Consultant

Dr. Carolyn Bridgemohan is board certified in developmental behavioral pediatrics and practices at the Developmental Medicine Center at Children's Hospital Boston. She is the director of the Autism Care Program and an assistant professor at Harvard Medical School. Her specialty areas are autism and other pervasive developmental disorders, developmental and learning problems, and developmental and behavioral pediatrics.